# Canticles of the Body

*Hapf
ge*

*Many blessings,
Cheryl Johnson
12/2018*

# Canticles of the Body

A Meditation on the Liturgical Cycle

Chris Ellery

RESOURCE *Publications* • Eugene, Oregon

CANTICLES OF THE BODY
A Meditation on the Liturgical Cycle

Resource Publications
An Imprint of Wipf and Stock Publishers
199 W. 8th Ave., Suite 3
Eugene, OR 97401

www.wipfandstock.com

PAPERBACK ISBN: 978-1-5326-5725-2
HARDCOVER ISBN: 978-1-5326-5726-9
EBOOK ISBN: 978-1-5326-5727-6

Manufactured in the U.S.A.                                    10/03/18

for Celia, body and soul

He took her by the hand and said, "Talitha cum," which means "Little girl, get up!"
—Mark 5:41 (NRSV)


Theologians may quarrel, but the mystics of the world speak the same language.
—Meister Eckhart

# Contents

# Acknowledgments

Many thanks to the editors of the following publications, in which some of these poems, many in slightly different versions and with different titles, first appeared:

*Blue Hole*

*Concho River Review*

*descant*

*The Enigmatist*

*Forrest Fest 2012*

*The Great American Wise Ass Poetry Anthology*

*Jewish Currents*

*Lilliput Review*

*The Lyric*

*One Person's Trash*

*Southern Poetry Anthology, Volume VIII: Texas*

*Switchgrass Review*

*The Texas Observer*

*Texas Poetry Calendar*

*The Unrorean*

*Voices de la Luna*

*Voices of Resilience*

*Windhover*

*Windward Review*

*Writing Texas*

"The Nativity of the Blessed Virgin Mary" (as "Birthday Poem"), "Palm Sunday," and "The Most Sacred Heart of Jesus" (as "Basic Anatomy of the Chest") are reprinted from *All This Light We Live In*, published by Panther Creek Press, 2006.

Under the title "Shekhinah," "Saint Andrew, Apostle" won the 2014 Alexander and Dora Raynes Poetry Competition, sponsored by *Jewish Currents*. It was first published in *Jewish Currents* and subsequently in the contest anthology, *Union: Poems by Forty Finalists from the 2014 Alexander and Dora Raynes Poetry Competition*. New York: Blue Thread Press, 2014.

"The Nativity of John the Baptist" was included by Fr. Richard Rohr, OFM, in his book *Eager to Love*. Cincinnati: Franciscan Media, 2014. It is impossible to overstate the influence of Fr. Richard on this collection, on my theology, and on my spiritual practice. I am deeply indebted to him for his teaching and writing and to all at the Center for Action and Contemplation for their selfless, loving, and inspired ministry.

The poems that draw from my travels to Syria and other countries of the Middle East are possible thanks to grants from the Council for the International Exchange of American Scholars and Angelo State University.

Hearty thanks to Matthew Wimer, my editor at Wipf and Stock, for all his insight and guidance, and to all at Wipf and Stock for their professionalism and dedication to their mission and ministry.

A tip of the sombrero and a big thank you to fellow members of the Texas Association of Creative Writing Teachers who responded to some of these poems as drafts, especially Jan Seale, Carol Reposa, and my fellow creative writing teachers at Angelo State University, Terry Dalrymple and Laurence Musgrove, good friends, partners in all my creative endeavors, and exemplary colleagues in every way. Many thanks also to Jeff Schonberg and Jeff Boone at ASU for walking me through some of these poems during our metaphysical workouts in the rec center—and on other occasions. I dare say the wheels of our recumbent bikes have not spun in vain.

And a thousand and one moon-drenched thank-yous to my buddy Glenn Cochran, wild mythologist and Walnut Mountain mystic. He has held the course with me through a thrilling voyage, and his big, wild heart beats in all the metrics of these verses.

I can only begin to sound the depth of my appreciation for my family. Their voices harmonize in these pages, beginning with Mom and Dad and my siblings, Linda, Chan, and Chuck. The sediment of their love is the bedrock of my faith. Next, I offer warm hugs and loving thanks to my beloved children and grandchildren: Sarah (Magistra, thank you for the Latin lessons and the many hours of music!), Benjamin, Elizabeth, Becca, Randy,

Parker, Alavehy, and McKayla. Beholding Christ in these dear and dazzling saints, I need no further evidence that love is the image of Love and being the likeness of Being. Above all, I give thanks, eternally, to Celia—my wife, best friend, fellow sojourner, priest, and superior self—for her magical way, which instills every moment with liturgical significance and makes all our life together one beautiful canticle of joy.

# Invocation

Last and first, always, to Divine Mind, the Beloved, Maker of All, Who sweetens and sustains my life with poetry and so much else, I offer this gaze of meditation in humble gratitude, for the grace of all that is good and wise in these poems and for the pardon of all that is vain.

Ever singing of changeless Love, I follow the Lord of Life.

## Introit: Body and Soul

The swami said to the soul:
"Only the unchangeable is real."
Immutable soul was overjoyed
and pitied flesh, which dies.
"Poor grass, poor flower, born
by human will to bloom a day,
to want and need and grasp,
to suffer pain through but a few
score years of strife and change,
to lose your rosy bloom in ash."

Flesh replied:
                    "Brevity
is my glory. From the sowing
of the seed, I pass through water
into light with lungs to cry,
with lips to suck the soft bud
of the breast, with blood to make
a child, with arms to hold
and ears to know her laughter,
a tongue to taste the honey
of his mother's love. Yes,
hour by hour I change,
and I will fade in hoariness
and rot, while you forever are.

Be it so.
Your more is Bliss.
My less is Joy."

# Advent
## Root and Ground

# Advent

"Sleeper, awake!
Rise from the dead,
and Christ will shine on you."

      —Eph 5:14b (NRSV)


Reckoning Easter moons by Golden Numbers,
the Book of Common Prayer promises
this bright December star will come again.
Fresh-washed in pews, hands folded—
intercession, confession, Annunciation—
we boys (the sons of men) peep
at the cherub-cheeked daughters of the parish.

The Advent hymns pour down from ages;
centuries of saints are with us here
to sing glad tidings of the Lamb of God
and King of kings. Canticles of praise
and welcome swell again so sweetly on
the Christmas lips of these we ogle.
"O come, O come, Emmanuel!"

Forced here by frowning women, fathers
thump our ears when we belch or snicker.
That sting, no more than could a reptile's bite,
cannot envenom our adoration.
Our hearts are open, our desires are known.
*Magnificat*—O wondrous conception!
*My soul proclaims the greatness.*

And you, little one, come by a girl's womb
to the cold stone world, *thou* who
*knowest* how every flower *fleeth*, surely
in your omniscience know our reverence—
that passion immaculate conceived in us,
for which we even now
prepare a way, a throne, a crown.

# Saint Andrew, Apostle

The spring of 1947, you
could smell catastrophe like rotting meat
in every quarter. In the scorching afternoons,
the old city dozed like a hungry cur, and when
we played together, Jews and Arabs, even our
football matches grew political. Because
we have the same birthday, Jamil said we
are twins. The father of his father made
the most ambrosial pizza in Bethlehem,
and often while I waited for my friend
to finish sweeping, he would tease his sweet
old *jedd*, Abdul-Salam, commanding him
like a great and ageless jinn to grant
a slice—tomatoes from his garden, cheese
from his own goats, oregano and mint,
the very flavor of bliss.
                              When Eema fell sick,
Jamil proposed we make *du'a* for her
at sacred Al Aqsa on the Temple Mount.
"But Jews can't go," I said. "Details, details,"
he grinned, and putting my *kippah* on he dropped
his white *taquiya* on this head of mine:
"Look at me I'm Jewish now, and you are Muslim."
I hope the ancient stones can still recall
our laughter as I chased Jamil from there
to the Church of the Nativity.

                              Since then
in dreams, like Cain, the foremost archetype
of brothers, I sometimes chase my brother still—
all the way to Jerusalem, where he died

in the first offensive. *May the memory*
*of the righteous be a blessing.* My brother knew
the Noble Qur'an by heart, as he knew
every alley and lane in the City of David.

## Saint Nicholas

Mee-mow
sleeps on my lap,
a coil of affection.
From deep in her
muscular
voice, her purring
climbs my spine
and opens a door
to heaven.

In the languor
of her love
I recall a kitten,
a gift one Christmas.
A few ounces of fur
and claws and whiskers,
a wisp of carbon
roughly the heft
of my heart.

# The Immaculate Conception of the Blessed Virgin Mary

The climax of the Sonora Caverns tour
is that moment in the Devil's Pit
when they turn the lights off to demonstrate
Total Darkness.

The guide had warned us. Even so
the limestone floor fell away,
a few girls screamed, and I am pretty sure
I heard Mrs. Townsend hyperventilate.

On the way back up, everyone joked
about it, and by the time we came out of the cave
we'd all been unafraid in that black world
deeper than blindness.

My eyes were barely adjusted to the sun
when Dusty grabbed me by the neck, my best friend
since first grade, and whispered what he'd done
right next to Doris Faraday.

Then some of us were poking around
in the gift shop buying postcards of the famous
Butterfly (it took a billion years
to grow its wings), and some were milling

around the bus, waiting for Mrs. Townsend
to bark us aboard for the drive back to Eden High.
Jack Jackson punched Fred Sorrel's arm
with his knuckle, Judy Willis stuck out her tongue

at Jordan James, like a mole coming out

of its burrow. There is proof
how quick the body can be
in the crystalline deep

of its metamorphosis.
Moon Milk Falls, White Giants,
Palace of Angels.
Beside the bus, Doris Faraday has her arms crossed

under her breasts,
and she's talking to three of her friends,
calm as water dripping, all of them unaware
just how intently Dusty and I are staring.

# Nuestra Señora de Guadalupe

Above the misty valleys of the Aztecs,
above the iron gates of the Conquerors,
the flowers of Tepayac whisper, the roses
that have never been trodden whisper
to all the downtrodden of the Americas.

The ones who are utterly defeated,
so lost they have forsaken desire,
have ears for the voice of their power—
a girl, a mother, an apparition
more substantial than the walls of a fortress.

"Make a vault of your body," she says,
"for the gold you are really seeking.
Carve a womb in your poverty
to receive the radiant Majesty,
which only the pure soul can conceive."

## Saint Lucy, Virgin and Martyr

Make a home in your mind
for the darkest and worst among us:
marauders, murderers, tyrants,
the ones who set off bombs in busy markets,
the ones who torture for pleasure,
the ones who rape and abuse,
the ones who prey on children.

Deranged, violent, lost,
caught in the coils
of their darkness,
they have made themselves
enemies of the body.

Have you light enough to love them?
Can you see
to fit inside yourself
a mercy to save them?
Here are my eyes.
Climb the tree where I am,
take my crown, and see,
as I see,
now.

# Saint John of the Cross

1.

The first idea in mind
is mouth of creation.
The infinite void.
The pregnant gloom.
Wind before voice, voice before light.
Light is motion of mind.
Inside are no edges of time.
Crossing day and night,
I taste the many shapes of hunger.
Crossing flux and repose,
I hear the prior silence of Word.

2.

I see
from my windowless cell
dust and smoke rising on a far hill.
Armies kill and die, die and kill.
Shouts and groans, the smell of death.
The poor remain poor, and the sour breath
of their deprivation
pierces the walls of my skull.

## 3.

I see
on a crowded street of Castile

a beggar child almost trampled
by the baron's horse.

A flash from the golden buckle
of one shoe scrapes my eyes.

The horse shies, the crowd laughs,
the man takes a whip to the girl.

His face is the mask of my pride.
Her mask is the face of my craving.

## 4.

When Gonzalo was a boy,
his father and uncles took him hunting.
To their joy, the first arrow of his quiver
found the throat of a majestic hart.

As he watched it bleed and die,
he saw the stag was watching him.
"My son, that venison
was my first taste of grief and glory."

When Gonzalo grew old enough to choose
his heart's desire, he remembered
the animal blood on the ground
and chose wisely.

5.

*Go with your feet bare.*
*Let the breath of the earth*
*enter you from below.*

Now, Beloved, I trust
there is life in even these stones
and room in my little womb
for all that You have thought and made.
Guide my soles through utter gloom
to feel Your way.

6.

On the road to Toledo
we were famished.
Conceive in your heart a mother
with nothing to nourish her son
save prayers for mercy.
Catalina fed my ears with a song
of her own devising,
a Goliard canticle of a boy and girl
who meet and love
and are forever happy.

7.

You Whom I seek in the darkness,
You, here, calling my weakness,
is it You who will take her from me,
the love my dear Gonzalo chose,
mother of my body and soul?
Say, is it You?

## In the flame

of my little lamp, I see her burning,
fever and tears in the endless night,
blood in her spittle,
and all my prayers ineffectual.

Why will You not listen to the cry
of my deepest desire flooding the dark?
From the bare cupboard of faith
Catalina fed her starving son
a way to know all space, out and in.

O cruelest Mystery, what can You offer my soul
from where You are hiding?


8.

My wise and dear Teresa, once a child,
is woman now in the animal way of time.
My body can never forget nor all her holiness hide
her body's loveliness from mine.
This manna feeds and refreshes all I am,
beast and essence, priest and man.

*Happy are those who can hunger and wonder.*
*Happy are those who suffer and learn.*


9.

My brothers, you brought me to this keep,
and in your pain meant pain for me.
Yet to our only Light I plead, O let light be
so that the good you truly are you truly see.

In the night and terror of your good,
Love made a pattern in my brain.
It grew until my emptiness was filled
and all my loss was gain.

## Christmas Eve

At church that Christmas Eve we heard again
how angels called the shepherds to the crib,
and coming home to nightly news we learned
that Santa had already left the Pole.

Carols, cocoa, a peek out front to the clear
snow-covered stretch of yard where deer
were sure to land, then off we're sent to bed.
My brother Mike was then the worldly age

of six. Suspicious of all myth, he lay
awake in winter restlessness to test
the truth of Santa's tricks. He woke me up—
I then was four—to swear our father placed

those sweets and toys beneath the tree.
I do not know
why I believed this boy that sometimes beat
me up, but did.
                        And even now that faith

amazes me—the fresh-faced kid, so brave
and so divinely cynical, the pure
delight of revelation in his voice
when he disturbed my easeful sleep.

# Christmas and Epiphany
## Our Special Abode

## The Nativity of the Lord

Ever-questing star, far night-wandering comet, or eclipse,
or strange stray planets alight, aligned, stop, stay,
hover here; rest, restless light, and shine. Love dips here, drips
bright beams from heaven-high earth-down on stable hay.

Your journey and the long nine months are done. Sighs some
jealous priest, some callous king. Fear not their fire, hot hate's dire whim.
Come, curious shepherds. Myrrh-smelling men, bestir and come
camel-back and wonder-wise to Bethlehem.

Behold what ass and lamb, beast-eyed, can see
swaddled at earth's breast, crèche—Love's child, Love's lord.
Let your manger-mind awake, O stranger self, and be
blessed guest, fresh-hallowed host, the flesh made word.

# Saint Stephen, the First Martyr

In the parish of sorrow,
the communicants themselves
are the bread of sacrament,
each torn piece
a witness of ritual
incomprehensible
to power and violence,
a feast
for the ones whose souls
are poured into iron coffins.

When the cup of that supper is passed,
let those who broke our bodies drink.
The high air of heaven rushes to earth
and iron doors fly open.

## Saint John, Apostle and Evangelist

Go into the darkest night, into the desert.
You cannot see the stones you kick

and stumble over or the gold beneath them.
You can feel the eyes of jackals

from the shadowy dunes as your pupils open
to all to which light blinds you. Dark matter,

dark thought, impossible and fatal love.
On that ground, let the gravity

of night pull you to a high place,
a hollow place, a stony place in the midst

of a garden, under the nimbus
of sacred dawn.

# The Holy Innocents

Calf and lamb and human child—
the mouth of every innocent
is seeking mother's breast.
Uncouth, unwashed, half-wild,
amazed, the restless shepherds press
to see the new-born light.
The burden he will bear these beasts
already know. In gifts and feasts
spread out for him a false god, grim,
is worshipped. No king can trace
straight lines upon the earth to face
his manger. Castles of the west,
to serve this prince, still haste
to send forth Herod's sword
to slaughter slaves whose Prophet cast
all idols from the sacred place
yet left this mother with her lord.
Even so, through sullen years
and from all lands, the magi hark
to hear the word that suckles here
and seek in milk of love that sun, the star
that overwhelms the dark.

## The Holy Family

In the mud house where we have learned to live
together, love is becoming Love.
Light and heat fuse all the particles.
We can see how it is
when we spread fresh sheets on the bed
or pour wine or listen to our children
making music with sticks and strings.
Cracks, of course, can open in the plaster.
Mold might grow as thick as sadness.
Boards will burn like so much paper.
Body and blood, we are not afraid.
Our charity overwhelms all that
and knows us for what we are, day
and night, what we have always been.

## The Solemnity of Mary
## or
## The Octave of the Nativity

"Tiger," "hawk,"
"serpent," "hog"—
in the old myth,
Adam gives names
to all he sees.
A bone becomes Eve.

Birth delivers breath,
which comes
and goes
circumscribed in all,
itself
uncircumscribed.

When a man
points to the sky
and mutters "thunderclap"
or "nimbus cloud,"
do not believe
his finger brings the rain.

# Epiphany

At the Majestic Theatre to see *Les Misérables*,
my daughter chats with a couple in the queue.
The man, loquacious with Sir Toby Belch's abs,
reveals that he rode down from Birmingham to view
the London premiere when 2-4-6-0-1
from France first broke parole in English song,
reflecting how it surely is remarkable
that for so long Monsieur Le Maire has dodged
Inspector Javert, his old antagonist and judge.

After the songs of destiny and redemption, after
the finale with ghosts and angels, tears and laughter,
along the new year's River Walk the trees still glisten
with Christmas lights beneath the Twelfth Night sky,
starry sky, that old symbol of eternity.
The river is black, and I think I finally comprehend
why Javert jumped. A leap terminates every obsession,
though day to day, good or bad, you cannot know the end.
Something the jolly man from England said: "A passion

of mine, dear girl, when I was a lad, was your story of the Alamo.
I itched to see where heroes died so made
my journey to this town and, what do you know,
met this sweet lady, and I stayed."

# Ordinary Time before Lent
## The Jeweled City

# The Baptism of Jesus

So this is it? This is what we crossed
a wilderness to see, risking death
by sun-stroke, thirst, and bandits? Just this?
Some wild Neanderthal with sun-burned face
and flecks of insects in his teeth, wearing a dress
of dromedary skins, dunking his next of kin?

Yes, there was that peal of thunder in
a cloudless sky, and one who had a better view
than I had claimed a ghostly bird appeared
above the scene when he went under. But I
saw only ripples on a muddy river
and water dripping when he broke the surface.
Now just like that he's gone, and who knows where,
and his crazy camel-coated cousin is back there
by the water where we left him muttering over
and over, "I am unworthy, unworthy, unworthy."
Night falls, and we depart dissatisfied and weary.

What can we say to those who sent us
to justify this costly caravan
and the hazard to so many learned men?
Nothing happened, that's a fact. No parting
of the waters, no column of fire. We can't invent
what we didn't see. And wouldn't I feel foolish
if I tried to say how still the earth seems now
as we travel home under a silver crescent
and how—somehow—in this shadowy, cold,
and barren land, everything looks different?

# Saint Anthony, Hermit and Abbot

Many like me in this pharaoh world
of arenas and TVs, deals and deeds,
have left all they had and all that had them
for the hermetic ether of a desert cavern.

Inside is the floor to which all libations flow
and the door of causation.
                              Carry no lantern
if you decide to go down to the hollow dark
where art first became a necessity.

Cloistered in the alchemy of your blindness
you will find the moon of every tide, the sun
to which all the flowers of your being turn.

## Saint Agnes, Virgin and Martyr

She was barely conscious
of her pubescent partner,
third string on the JV team
with acne
earnestly holding the book,
pointing to the diagram,
and reading the words
that named the things
they should find inside.
ESOPHAGUS ATRIUM EGGS OVIDUCT.
She was holding the scalpel.
The teacher came and laid the frog
on the tray in front of her.
She had never seen anything
so naked,
supine and helpless—
the cadaverous skin nearly human,
legs splayed,
like a sleeping baby,
like a skydiver seen from below
falling.
Where would it go if the chute didn't open?
What would it be if dogs ate the body?
Then she heard
from across the room,
"The word cereal comes from Ceres,
the Roman goddess of grain."
It was totally random,
out of context,
that amphibious lapping of midnight water
on sunlit fields of ripening wheat.

But that's how it is.
Suddenly just *here*.
Certain as winter.
Certain as spring.
The friction of two facts
flaring
in the starless underworld
changes everything,
like fire and flesh
and rain.

# The Conversion of Saint Paul, Apostle

"The devil of letters beholds the All in slivers of AUM
and comes to the Shining City breathing murder."

Halfway through the corkscrew journey
of my pyramid-plotted life,
I reached a turning. A son was born
to me. It was my choice to have him
circumcised—a matter of health
and hygiene, said our gentile
pediatrician. This elective surgery
involved a plastic ring, and when
eight days had passed, a circle of
necrotic skin fell off in his diaper.
Every Hebrew man bears
on his body the scar of covenant.

"One like lightning knocked me to the level
of the lowest wheel, down to the wormy roots
of darkness. For three days I was deep in death.
He showed me all my suffering then spoke
his *talitha cum* to my soul. And it came rising."

She labored three long days
with him until the obstetrician
saw him crowning. I coached
my wife to breathe and cursed
my deity for her agony.
Then, at last, they cut her womb
and plucked him out.

Must we remember all the traumas

of infancy? My father was also
thirty-five (our body's age
in Paradise, I'm told) when I,
his ultimate son, was born. I seem
to hear the cries of my newborn soul
when I was circumcised. One time
I saw my father die before he died.
We were playing on the floor,
I tickled him until he laughed
so hard he just quit breathing.
I do not know how long we lay
in silence, but long enough to kiss
the dust and give our cheeks to the Smiter.
Many kingdoms rose and fell
as I was tumbling down to Sheol,
and when at last he breathed again
I swear that both of us were changed.

A little bridle holds the breath
to the body's twisting shaft.
Just sever this and life will go.
Adroit centurions of Rome
perfected the art of crucifixion
for torture and execution.
One theory says the victim
dies from asphyxiation.
Reserved for Roman citizens,
decapitation is an equally
effective means of stopping breath.

Every breath is a conversion,
the exchange of gases.
Conversion is a laughing matter.

> "From the exile of religion he called me back to be myself,
> to walk a little way with him, a slave no more.
> I was going that way, now I'm going this.
>
> *Shema Yisrael*

*Adhonai Elohenu*
*Adhonai Echad*

With a spear in my prayers, I set out for the Shining City.
With my eyes full of light, I leave these walls breathing *hessed*."

# Candlemas
## or
## The Presentation of the Lord

In the bathroom closet where
the cat gave birth, my mother kept
her Kotex. A white rose bloomed
on the blue box. At five years old
I could not read the words or catch
the incantation: "Feminine Napkins."
"Deep Downy Soft Impressions."
How could I understand the blood
that stained them every month
even as I watched those kittens
being born—feeble, wet, and blind?
Inside the pitch-dark room (the door
shut tight) I held a penlight on
each one and named them as
they came: there was Blackie, Dottie,
Alex, Rocky, Barney, Fred,
and Tom, which was the one born dead.

# Saint Agatha, Virgin and Martyr

If I were a daisy I know I'd be crazy
For honeybee bellies and hummingbird noses.
I'd open my beauty on days warm and lazy
With sunflowers, clover, wild posies and roses.

If I were a raindrop I'd drop with my friends
Through dark icy clouds and lightning flashes.
We'd gleefully ride where the rainbow bends
Refreshing the earth with miraculous splashes.

If I were the sunshine I'd kiss all the faces
Of beetles and eagles, meadows and streams.
I'd burst into color where the raindrop races
And whisper goodnight with my last golden beams.

Now, I'm not the sun or a droplet or flower.
I am only me with my wee hands and feet.
Still I give all my beauty and use all my power
To love all I see with my heart free and sweet.

# The Confession of Saint Peter, Apostle

To give the fish
we brought home alive
a quick death,
my uncle taught me
to punch the knife in
just above
and just behind
the eye.
         Taut twitch,
muscular fish,
prick of fins,
wild arc
of her wide graceful tail,
tense against
what pinned her
to the board.

"Fish don't feel no pain,"
my uncle said.
"It thinks it's still
in the lake
just swimming away."

Scales and spine.
Guts and bones
and yellow spawn.
Gills twitching
on the severed heads,
the dead eyes
black and bottomless.

Later, in my bed,
in the deep of my sleep,
my uncle caught me.
My boneless body,
taut, caught
in the muddy flesh
of his arms.
Still alive, I think,
when he stabbed me,
I fought, I fought
to swim away in the watery dark.

## Shrove Tuesday

Full of grace the god of war
anoints his idiot as king.
The sun withdraws his gravity,
so floats the Fool. *All hail his reign!*
Ordained by him all upside down
this one fat day the lioness
tops the lion, trampled fish
gobble up the swine, hawk
kisses mouse, and comes
the glad old dragon of the East
puffing merriment, his laugh
unleashed, mask over mouth,
in loud and carnal psalteries,
in blessings for the plumed
and painted boys and maids.
The Rainbow, blasted,
drips color to the street.
Dolphin, bird, boa, pearl,
all corporeal seeds of earth
meet in the wild feast.
Skin so quick ahead of shrift
perceives the daily dragon in us all:
our red religious snarls,
our bloated, black, despotic leers
so blind to being's loveliness,
to flesh alive (*forgive us
lord for we have sinned*) here
below the icy heat of stars.

# Lent and Holy Week
## Unstuck

# Ash Wednesday

When Mr. Armstrong got the news
he came straight over
and told my mother
then went back to his painting.

Momma changed
her clothes then went next door
to comfort her neighbor.
We walked right in.

There was Mr. Armstrong
painting the living room.
The room was empty,
hollow-sounding, and on the floor
paint-spackled canvas caught
the droplets—I can't tell you the color.

I saw the yellow kittens
frisking at the feet
of Mr. Armstrong's ladder, darting
in and out of a hole
made by a fold in the canvas.

That house made not a sound
to say their son
was dead in Vietnam. In the den,
the TV was on
the same as always, the same
soap opera my mother
had been watching.
Miz Armstrong stared

at a couple fighting.

Momma asked, "Sharon how are you?"
Miz Armstrong had no answer.

Momma seemed to think
some kind of silence needed filling
so with her arm around
Miz Armstrong's shoulder
asked how it happened, where and when.

Miz Armstrong tried to tell
but when she spoke could not approach
the heat and smoke
of that body burning.

I kept thinking about the kittens
and Mr. Armstrong on the ladder
with a rag in his back pocket.
Nothing about it seemed natural

until a scream
like a cat's tail being stepped on.
We all rushed in
where Mr. Armstrong had been painting.

He said, "It was under the tarp."
He said, "I just stepped down from the ladder."

He was cradling the dead kitten
in a white rag. A little blood
flaring on that shroud
engulfed the whole house.

# Lent

Months of scourging drought and scorching sun,
now April lightning sets our county ablaze.
Dozers, choppers, exhausted women and men
battle the raging wildcat fires for days.

High noon is a dirty smudge of light.
Lungs clench in smoke-filled air. Relentless wind
is driving the fires toward town. On the third night,
evacuation sirens pierce our nightmares of the world's end.

Yet we wake not to panic, but a thrill
of love, neighbor helping neighbor, flares in the loss
and letting go. Having seen this miracle,
we rush to wait for new life in the ash.

# Saint Joseph, Spouse of the Blessed Virgin Mary

At home among the gruff and storm-worn shepherds,
she sang to calm the sheep at lambing time,
and when one bleated in distress, she reached
inside to guide the little feet into the light.
Laying the new-born lamb along the fleece,
she grinned and slung the mucous from her hands
then patted the flanks of the exhausted ewe.

Seeing her I could believe my manhood
something good, so that coupled with the energies
of womanhood it might serve God.
Still, before I bargained for her hand,
I knew her will. She was the one to choose.
So I framed for her a perfect house,
dove-tailed a perfect cradle for our sons.

Chaos lashed me, law shrieked, bitter and hard
as bloody death. Outside the gate I went
to gather stones and waited in the fire
for her to come. Her face rose up to me,
lotus sweet, white as any lamb
that heir of Aaron ever put to knife
upon the altar of our fathers' faith.

I dropped my stone and nailed my anger to a tree.
In the one who bore me to a better self,
the seed of resurrection has been sown.
I take that blessed body for my own.

# The Annunciation

Can I cry my no before the awesome messenger of light?
Can I refuse my blood-rich uterus?
Can I argue my love by denying my womb,
the zero through which all men must pass?

I have seen the frenzy
in fields and cities, life killing life.
It should not be.
I know my body is the door of death.

He enters me like a fish. I must say yes.
His favor masters my virgin will.
Letting go I behold
the dance of life redeemed and beautiful.

Who sees under my heart
inside the three-sided room
where three-sided God is taking form?

I could not love you in my own way, my son.
What I can do, I do.
In the spongy ocean of myself,
for a little while I cradle you.

# Palm Sunday

One winter then another their remains
have waited for this spring
in the crematory vault
while we next-of-kin fought
about the final resting place.
Alive, they voiced no slightest trace
of preference;
it was a matter of indifference
whether to scatter the bits or bury them
or lock their dust in a columbarium.
It's only ash and bone,
they said. But some of us wanted a stone,
a marker, and a place to come,
to sit and say, "They're home."

A half a year we spent
debating, another passed before their monument
could be quarried, carved, engraved, and yet
one more till we could get
the busy clan together, postponing life—
jobs, school, chemo for one brother's wife—
long enough to sink a spade
in the soft soil where shade
spreads over a knoll near Buffalo Creek.

Thus, at last, we meet this week
before Easter to attend to the long-neglected chore.
They are with us once more
as we discuss how deep to dig.
The bags that hold them are not big,
and ashes have no smell that would attract

a prowling pack.
Not very deep, the elders say.
So pushing the shovel in the clay
I dig until the earth itself
dictates the depth to a stony shelf.
Not very deep.
But plenty deep enough to keep
their gray remnants forever from the sun.

We pour them in.
Not them. We pour the ashes in.
A slight cloud rises in the hole. We wait
for it to settle, list a beat,
water and wind,
and for the first time look beyond
that grassy hillside flecked with graves
to the meadow just beyond, to the blue hills fading into haze.

# Maundy Thursday

Tapestry of *The Last Supper*
in the cafeteria of the private academy.
One alone in the middle of this art.
Iconic apostles, awed—each declaims
a world of governors. Outside the drab
upper room, lovers reach agreements,
and even the frogs squat contentedly
by the pool where lepers wash.

# Good Friday

When the table is set with the sins of man
it never fails to yield a feast. My beak
is sharp enough to reach the tastiest liver.
But my palate's not particular.
The bowels of this messiah or his thigh
will do to satisfy my appetite.
Furthermore, as I suppose you know,
there is no scarcity of pickings on
this hill, so I've already broken fast
today. Meanwhile, it is good exercise
to fly in circles. Therefore, Roman, drive
the nails in at your leisure. Feel free
to hesitate between each hammer blow
and gaze upon his face with pleasure.
Enjoy the grimace of all crime, relish
the scream of all rebellion in one body.
No cause to rush on my account, for I'm
not squeamish about dining on the Sabbath.
In my cult it is completely kosher. No doubt
the rabble down there in the shadow of
my wings, hurling their vices at the man
with rocks and rotten figs, are in a hurry
to pass their knives across the throats of lambs,
to roast the meat with endives and horseradish,
and to light menorahs. They have no time for him
to suffocate. One reason more, I guess,
to draw to draw to draw it out. Am I correct?
Still, perhaps your mistress waits for you
to come. I doubt our Prefect with
his well-scrubbed hands will much object if you
decide to hasten his last breath a bit.

Break his legs, therefore. Skewer this "lord"
with spear. Unsheathe your sword and pierce his side
to expedite my evening meal with a sauce
of blood and bile. Surely Jove will bless
you for your mercy to both man and mob.
By all means, then, impale that so-called king
before the sun can set. Twist your weapon
in his guts and leave the ripe fruit hanging
on the tree.
                    What? Has he already died?
Verily, you are an artist, sir, and pillar
of all good. Centuries to come
may carve and paint and write this scene below
the words *Behold, the man!* But not a hand
can ever possibly approximate
the archetype, your masterpiece. *Ergo,*
from my heart, I say, Centurion,
with unequivocal respect, "*Laus omnis
sit tibi pro beneficiis tuis.*"

## Holy Saturday

On Saturdays I walk to Fairmont Park
to see Saint Francis and the grave of a friend.
Real doves befriend bronze doves
in Frankie's arms. I sit on a broken concrete bench.

No one is digging this early here.
Here in the shade, the sun just up,
it seems easy enough to renounce desire,
to refuse a father's world and wealth,

ambition, power, sex for his green life
of loving birds. My friend lies near.
Madelle, a dentist's widow, now
unconsciously collected here, has left

behind a fine house on the river,
books by Dante, books on Dante,
copious notes from lectures on Jung.
She too touched living things as if divine.

Man or woman, then or now—
each may choose
a certain habit, handle feathers, thoughts,
finish in the same bright silence.

# The Great Vigil of Easter

Behind your house there is a lake.
You probably can't see it.
Carry your fear to the edge and throw it in.

That stone will open a mouth in the water:
*Suffering suffering I am great suffering*
*I am all the world's suffering.*

Kneel at the shore of that lake.
Cup your hand, and taste the water.
Know yourself for the very first time.

# Easter
## The Pure Soul

# The Resurrection

One day
soon
when you are most distracted
by light or music
I will sneak under your joy,
a droplet,
and enter you
there where your grandmother's stories pierced you,
opened you wider than understanding,
deeper than remembering,
and there, under your joy, I will rest in readiness
as long as you live
and be
the courage you could never imagine in mountains,
the calm in a comet's tail when you need it,
your kindness, ripe with compassion, bowing
like pine to the sky,
like night to a white dress,
as a child in rags, putting hands together, smiling,
bows
with utmost respect and equality
to a fellow deity.

## Saint Mark, Evangelist and Martyr

When I was young and scared
they seized me. I slipped
from my old clothes and ran away,
bare. Banished,

I copied every letter
of my father's body.
What moved above the waters
moves in his story.

O whoever has ears, listen!
May the Lion that roars
in every stroke—light and power
of every flame—soar inside you.

## Sunday of Divine Mercy

The doctor asked me to bend
my son in half and hold him
very still while he drew
fluid from his spine
to check for meningitis.
In the afternoon we drove
up Mount Nebo on clear roads
to find the pine needles
coated with ice.

# Saint Philip and Saint James, Apostles

They walked into town at sunset,
two without baggage or ration.
Convicts we thought them, bound
for the cities of refuge.

They looked at the *shohet*, the butcher,
a severe, unsociable man
grieving the loss of his daughter.
He offered them hospitality.

They soon began to teach.
"See," they said, "see it
spread out even now on earth,
in the print of your unlived lives."

First we saw only our shadows
in the silhouettes of their white robes.
"Look within," they said. "It is there."

In the morning the butcher was singing as
across the lamb's white throat
he drew his knife.

Lightning flared on the blade.
We heard the two sounds of thunder:
the rumble, crack, and boom of sky splitting
and the silence that follows.

For three days we listened
to these men without cloaks or houses,
no self to empty or lose.

When they left, they took nothing—
nothing save the dust on their shoes.

# The Good Shepherd

*Elegy for Father Frans*
*d. April 7, 2014*
*Homs, Syria*

Where the mind is led forward by Thee, into ever-widening thought and action—into that heaven of freedom, Father, let my country awake.

—Rabindranath Tagore, *Gitanjali*


This year at Easter
there is snow
on the Llano Estacado.
It dabs my roses with white.
It dusts the green vineyards of my neighbors.
It drifts across the mesas,
powdering the grasses,
whitening the air above the Staked Plains.

Above the high escarpment of the Caprock
a pure brightness
lifts me again
to my Syrian mountains.
On my last long walk before the civil war
chased me from Syria,
I followed Father Frans
across the Anti-Lebanon.

We were men and women hiking.
Arab, Alawite, Armenian, American

traipsing after the Dutch pastor
in the tracks of his vigorous hope.
"Christians, Muslims.
All I see are human beings."
A week after a blizzard
buried Homs and Damascus

snow still filled the crevices and passes.
You could not find your path
anywhere in the mountains.
It seemed so foolish, freezing.
It seemed so what it seems
to be led by a madman.
But there ahead of us walked Father Frans,
assured and humorous, tranquil and cheering.

Too blinded with glare
to keep the thin line of his steps
I strayed into belly-deep drifts.
The wet snow chilled my bones and spirit.
At the height of my complaining
Father Frans stretched out his arms,
turning, as if to hold every vista
I was busy not seeing: "When, when

will you ever again see such horizons?"
Westward the Great Sea, to the east
Damascus. That way, northwest,
the Beqaa Valley—Baalbeck,
the Heliopolis, with its many deities.
And over there, Mount Herman,
Jabal al Shaykh to the Arabs,
the ancient Golan, once a city of refuge.

In every direction, white peaks
stretched toward the blue infinity.
He patted my shoulder, smiling,
and surging ahead in the feathery light,

advancing toward a vague whiteness,
he left me this: "One who is suffering
cannot see beauty. But if you miss this moment,
how will you remember?"

A year now
since veiled assassins
came at night to lead the old priest
where he did not want to go,
I see his picture on the Internet.
It is snowing in Texas.
Easter again, and the devil
is still spreading gore all over Syria,

a land so bathed in violence
that we call a favorite flower
Blood of Martyrs.
I stare at his corpse in the casket.
I stare at the pixels
until his face, pale and stricken,
is the face of all the crucified,
every sect and nation.

He opens his eyes.
He smiles and rises.
He sheds his vestments, sheds the cloth
that wraps the wounds of his execution.
Standing now, eager to set out,
he drapes his crown
with the red and white *kheffiyeh*,
for he was Syrian.

*We all are Syrian.*
*All. All.*
*All fragile. Bone and blood. Mind and spirit.*
*Susceptible to hate, division.*
*Sudden, senseless killing.*

Snow has come like a benediction,
an unexpected lover.
The flowers in my garden, brightened,
have clarified their colors. The vines,
untouched by frost, seem lit from inside.
And the scrubby escarpment of the Estacado
is suddenly, somehow,
infinite.

Taking up his staff, a shepherd's staff,
Father Frans begins his pilgrimage.
A first step, and another
of what might be an endless journey.
On the way he beckons
to every child, every *imago dei*: *Join us*.
To murdered and murderer: *Join us*.
To torturer and tortured: *Join*.

All follow the aged father
through parks and roundabouts,
villages, orchards,
crossing the red soil
of that ancient land,
ambling toward sunset
to the sparkling ozone, the clear breath
of the Anti-Lebanon.

Up and up
and across the snowy peaks
through heart-high drifts,
we joke and chatter.
We know our many wounds, received and given.
We know we go to some sacred valley.
And we are laughing,
for up ahead we see him laughing,

Pater Frans, advancing over ice
with his long sure strides

in the white bliss of his kindness.
Advancing, advancing
with light steps, with silent love.
In the pure passion
of egoless adoration,
advancing.

## Saint Matthias, Apostle

One night as we neared
Jerusalem we camped
in a stony garden.
The smothering air
kept me from sleeping.
Beside me, Judas
arose from his tossing
and turning. The Master
was gone. We were alone.
The disciples were snoring.

I followed my friend
out into the dark,
saying, "Brother,
what demon dream
has spoiled your sleep?"
I could see he was beaten,
sweating and trembling
as if all particles
and waves of light
were hurled against him.

"I am chosen," he said,
"to be for all time
the shadow
of Love's desiring."
He wept without weeping.

Finding no words,
I rested my hands
on his head

in benediction.
At last he said, "Return
to your rest, Matthias.
You too must choose
to be chosen."
Deeply distressed
I wandered the garden.

Turning and turning
his words in my mind
like a spade breaking soil
in a dry plot of ground,
I came upon the Master,
slumped under a fig tree.
Like Judas, he too
looked utterly beaten,
very image of death
and desolation.

The dark was deep,
and dawn seemed far
out of reach. Still,
as I crept away,
suddenly well-being
overflowed in me.
I found myself.
And all around me
in the night, the stars
and the stones were breathing.

## Saint Bede the Venerable

Stomping around in the Book of Genesis
I met an old Indian sage
resting at a well of the desert.

Having (so he said) no rope or vessel,
he asked me to bring up water.

As we satisfied thirst together
the flow of the wind obscured our steps
along with the tracks of camels and herds
and all who came before us. He said,

> "Sand can trap the print of our wandering
> but soon forgets its meaning."

Because I had an appointment in Canaan
I left him alone at the well
doing nothing.

After eons of drifting through stories
I met him again in the Book of Revelation.
He was washing his robe in a spring
at the gate of the Shining City.

I was astonished to see him alive,
but if he felt the least iota of surprise
it was imperceptible.

As he drew his robe from the water
I remembered all the times I was thirsty.

When he draped it around my body
it was already dry,
white as a cloud of the desert.

The pool where he had washed it
showed no trace of disturbance,
flowed

>without sediment.

He invited me to drink. I did.
Though he formed no words against the silence
clearly I could hear him speaking:

>"This water
>is the same water
>you gave me."

# The Visitation

for John and Laurie Norman

Atlas, who shoulders heaven with all its mansions,
by a goddess of ocean fathered Maia, first
of the Pleiades, who in turn conceived me
in the secrecy of night to all-mighty Father Zeus.
I am Hermes ...

—Euripides, *Ion*

## 1. Matins::Vow of Silence

Behold the hour cometh and now is
when all miscarried and aborted cry,
"O lucky stars! O fortunate demise!"
Mothers, eschew epidural and episiotomy.
Foolish fathers raise up foolish seed.
Though angry astrologers protest,
we know the never-born are blessed.
Birth is but disaster, and God dwells
in the vacuum of the aspirated womb.

In this hotel the walls are thin.
I hear two girls make love (Ah, love!)
with giggles and sighs. On HBO
a stiff and sprightly courtesy
is mouthed between a handsome prince
and shining knight. *O young fresh folks!*

I, Galahad, watch with sword and lance.
But why am I so favored that
the mother of my Lord should come
to delve in subtle matters of the heart?
Oh, vision blessed! From this night hence
the wombs I dream of drip with silence.


## 2. Lauds::Spell

Millennia before the birth
of Christ we Magi knew
the cyclic order of the stars.
Visitors of old revealed
to us the wonders of those lights
with all the festivals of the body's year.
All the *vedas* turn on a word.
I am ever burning fire,
I eternal Ganga's spring.


## 3. Prime::Tell

Tell Tuneinir, the Hill of Ovens.
These bones from which we brush the dirt
once held up human flesh—and will
again if what they say is true.
We dig their story bone by bone,
particles of atoms of molecules.
Their oil lamps broken in the dust
gleam in the darkness of the underworld.
Animal bones, flint sickle blades,
bits of crossbows, iron swords,
artifacts of war and peace and war
between the Tigris and Euphrates
where some say Eden was.
A flood is coming. The time draws near
when Chinese engineers will close

the gates of Khabur Dam. Therefore late
and early let us excavate.
Soon turbines high as citadels
will turn and turn and turn the waters
of this Paradise to light. We rest
at noon, suck pomegranate seeds
for strength, and sift the secrets of the tell
for clues to who we were and are
before the Khabur Reservoir can fill.
From here to Tadmor lines are strung.
A fierce sun burns the garden where we fell
generation after generation
to the many levels of this place.
Babylonian we have found,
and Byzantine, Assyrian,
Persian, Roman; temple, church, and mosque,
houses, market, bath, and monastery
bear their disasters to the sun again.
Not every visitor who comes
brings frankincense and myrrh and gold.
We write the tale on martyrs' bones.
The arc of their sickles and the sowing of grain.
The flash of their arrows and the raping of girls.
The blink of their cursors and the making of deals
between the Hudson and Potomac
on a given day. Dumb Grief
luxuriates in epitaphs
yet only silence tells the truth.
These Arab friends who dig and eat
and dance with us may be for all
we know remnants of the Exile,
descendants of Israel's lost tribes.
Seeds take root in the earth,
woman must give birth.
O deliver to us the flickering light,
that we might bear it through the night.

## 4. Terce::Babble

ain't you a little old
forty-five that's almost my granny's age
me i'm seventeen
you don't look too bad
it's nice to know you never get too old for it
heard lady gaga's into abstinence
says it's good for your health
yeah right to each her own i guess
that may well be one way to stay away
from this god-forsaken place
but it's not my way
what about you what brings you here
you afraid it'll be a retard
think you just too old to have a kid
you have any others
of course I know it's none of my business
but you look so scared thought you might want to talk
i can zip it if you want me to
mom's always saying i like to talk too much about
what can't be talked about
well then okay we'll talk
your first time here
don't worry this is my third
it's a piece of pie easy as cake
course i heard of birth control you think i'm dumb
i never remember to take them pills
and stupid me i can't say no
i love the boys i really do
i don't ever want to be a mom
i mean the world is wicked right
see this bruise
my daddy gave me that thanks very much
no he don't drink
he works in a bank and brags about his tithe
how could he raise such a slut that's what he said
dear old dad
but don't get the idea i'm acting out

yeah i know what that means
it ain't some daddy thing
see these earrings my friend maria gave me these
precious little latina girl
plays violin got a crucifix in her room
very sweet
for some reason she likes to hang with me
i did her brother mario once
right there in her room
skin as soft as a newborn soul to kiss
the taste of sunlight
gush of sunny oceans
jeez i hope she never finds out
in a few more weeks i'll be eighteen
i can get a job down at desiree's
exotic dancer i like to dance
i know this girl says she can get me on i've got the stats
already picked my stage name out cleopatra dunn ain't it sick
maybe i'll dance with snakes that'd be a kick
beth adams yeah i'm here alright
just keep your pants on give me a sec
well they're calling me i got to go
it's been real
good luck maybe i'll see you around
come may or june
stop by desiree's
catch my show


## 5. Sext::Protocol

a god
gives us
our hands
our hands
give us
the task
the task

                gives us
                our self

Our daughter turns eighteen today,
abroad a year in Germany.
We can visit peer to peer
by certain online protocols
that frankly I'm confounded by—
a fact which merely magnifies
my gratitude. I leap to see
the beaming pixels of her face
and know she's safe at least for now
there on the desktop monitor.

> *In Greece there have been riots,*
> *neo-Nazis in Berlin.*
> *Every windmill is a giant,*
> *the world is full of sin.*

No evil dims for her the thrill
of the old world. Spring break she went
to Paris to see her favorite,
Taylor Swift. Last week, Beethoven
in Venice. Next she'll visit Ephesus,
then Istanbul. What a crazy dance
we do these days with distance.

*Infans mirabilis* we like to say,
for I conceived her on the brink
of my old age, and Dr. Brooks,
my trusted gynecologist,
recited epic catalogues
of risks and scattered reasons in
my brain like seeds for why this dry
and withered pod should not bear fruit.
Yet not a grain of what he said
took root—and here she is, my choice,
my dear Elizabeth, this moon,

this leaf, this wave of all that is
or was or ever will exist.
"And how are you, my precious girl?"
A continent away she smiles,
winging quick as wisdom home.
Hence I believe in miracles
and say all space is luminous
and liminal, leading us
through oceanic tides to what will be.


## 6. None::Elegy

And so he died, and so she grieves.
The one she bore no more is breathing.
Earth its empty jar receives.
*The Absolute is pure Being.*

That day was like the night. No form
we think we see can seem a true thing.
This dust and ash, a quantum swarm.
*The Absolute is Nothing.*

In all your eulogies declare,
O daughter of the world, a fire transforming.
The lamp receives the light. O swear
*The Absolute is Becoming.*


## 7. Vespers::Psalm

Our faces are toward the sunset, Livy.
Who is this that darkens counsel?
*Deus, in adjutorium meum intende.*
Inside this engine, our beatitudes
have dried. The fly that we heard buzzing
at the window is dead on the sill.
It came with revelation and its voice

we heeded not. Tender is the night
alrighty. Light seeps under the door,
here on the eve of apocalypse,
and who is that winged one at the window?
All creatures do his bidding.
Visitation will begin at ten.
Rosary at seven.

*Glory to the Father and to the Son and to the Holy Spirit*
*as it was in the beginning, is now, and will be forever. Amen*

The lowliness of the maiden,
the mercy of generations.
An empty sleeve He fills with storm,
He breaks the pride of clay. The poor
in habits made of light He feasts.
On me His greatest favor rests.

> Goddess comes
> God-bearing girl,
> and I the son
> of woman born.
> In the turbine
> of my heart
> Thou hast gathered
> all the seas.
> Thrice blessed
> is Thy possession.
> Five loaves with wine
> and oil are blessed.
> Pisces in the fire,
> the harp's new string.

Now look Ye out on all the race of men.
Now let Thy servant leave in peace.

## 8. Compline::Buzz

Midway through the *Gazette* shift (3 p.m.
to midnight) Jonas at the City Desk
sends J.C., his copyboy, to Bruno's for
fried peanuts and a Texas Burger, hold
the onion, extra cheese. The high school kids
are hanging out, exchanging the usual
pleasantries. J.C. in his purple paisley tie
stands out. The people marveled that
he tarried so long in the temple. Back
at the City Desk again he writes
obituaries. Chain-smoking Jonas,
omnipotent among the liturgists,
insists the letter C in J.C. stands
for Cocksman, then he scurries to
the paste-up room with propositions for
the paste-up girls less honorable
than cherubim. A deep sleep fell
upon the man, and then all hell broke loose.

*Now the time came for Elizabeth to give birth,*
*and she bore a son.*

Page one of tomorrow's *Gazette* will say four children died
by hit and run, a suspect in the county jail. Intoxication
may or may not be involved, a spokesman for the Sheriff states.
Investigation is on-going now and surely will reveal the facts.
Taliban gunmen lay siege to Afghan hotel; 18 dead.
Guilty verdict reached by jury in child sex trial.
48 pica bfc for ye knew not the time of my visitation.
So we put yet another edition to bed and turn our thoughts to rest.

> Now I lay me down to sleep,
> Mr. Polytrope my soul to keep.
> *O Domina Theotokos nubilis!*
> In the third trimester of
> my junior year,
> I went down to Syria to dig

my ancient spear.

Benedict is my patron saint,
and Basil my eastern brother.
First sleep is always best sleep.
After that, there is no other.

A ruined chapel near the Basin of
Elijah, Mount Sinai. We kindle fire
against the cold and wait for light. We come
from Leipzig, Montreal, and Angelo.
To Moses' Cave with feathered feet we'll go
at dawn to watch another sun come up
where YHWH's finger gouged his stony law.
Phineas intervened. And it was reckoned
to him as righteousness. That poor old sister
still hawking her little bundle of words
and calling it enlightenment.

Beyond the dream of right or wrong,
beyond the walls of worthy or unworthy,
there is a field of ripening grain.
Sweet, young Fidel, he loved the hard line drive
and sprint to first. Now old and sick
and in the vise-strong grip of death
in watches of the night he dreams
not of the firing squads or bark
of seals but of the clean, dry dirt
at home when he slid safe from third.

> *O wake and watch! O watch and wait!*
> *A cunning thief comes by night,*
> *behold his wondrous deeds!*
> *Make straight his way!*

Everyone you meet everyone you meet everyone you meet
is fighting a big jihad.
*Lefty Loosy Righty Tighty.*

Werewolf, vampire, write that down
lest we forget
fang and throat are symbols.
I know my task, I know the labor set for me.
Love for no good reason.

> In the knot of an elder tree
> all the Universe I see.

I speak as to children not listening.
Flocks of false messiahs.
"Teacher, do you not care that we are perishing?"
"My teaching is not my own."

> Here in her decrepit womb
> I felt the ages turn and turn
> waiting for his fire to burn,
> waiting for the Immaculate to come.

> Timeless Hera guards my fetal sleep
> and his, who is both dark and light.
> Now deep in amniotic night
> I wake and leap!

## 9. Matins::Oral Tradition

On my little way I went into the forest
where my wound was deepest
where my shadow was darkest.
I charm the wounded serpent from her hole and hold until she heals.

## Rogation Days

Poverty encircles abundance,
choking joy within hedgerows of sorrow.
Falsehood and ignorance, guarding the borders,
prohibit truth from crossing.

When it builds a wall around its holdings,
love can expect a siege.
With trebuchet and mangonel,
hate launches stones and missiles at the holy city.

Hate's ally, Death, wraps the throat with iron hands.
Let every priest of the parish
walk the circumference, beat the bounds
with loving-kindness.

On every side, believer, sew more blessings
until the boundary spirals wider and wider, wide as creation expanding.
Until the harvest overfills the cosmos.
Until whoever was out is inside.

# The Ascension

Through walls of rain
we saw the wind
lift the trailer ahead
like a sheet of tin
from an old barn
and flip the 18-wheeler
in the ditch.

We pulled ahead
and stopped,
and when we saw him
saw enough
to think him just a thing.
But one of us
knew enough
to feel a pulse,
and it became
a man again.

For the long hour
it took to extricate
we fed him
soothing words
we didn't half believe.
The whole cab
pushed his head
into the mud.

Still we stroked
and patted the parts
of him we could—

a hand and foot—
and praised his vitals
and said the storm
had passed and what
a bitch it was,

and we could feel him
breathing away
while the jaws
of life cut steel,
and we knew how small
words are,
like drops of rain
from those high clouds
still spitting
on the crawling cars.

Once on the gurney
he was stripped—
jeans cut away
from hips
to find a vein—
and because the tube
could find no way
through his crushed face,
they opened his throat
in front of us.

When the helicopter
lifted him away,
we looked up
then down
from where he was
and saw ourselves
on the ground

left with nothing
but the wreck,

the broken cargo
spilled over the road,
bits of himself,
and a little blood
that had drained
into the ditch.

# Pentecost
## Theocracy

## Pentecost I

There is no wind this morning
which means the trees
are not moving their leaves.
That's just how it works
in this country:
first this then that.
You could call it the law.
Trees aren't allowed to move their leaves
without wind however much they will.
One day in a treehouse
I asked this older kid
what makes the wind?
He said the sun burns the air
and the unburned air rushes in.
He was big:
I believed him for many years.
I liked believing. It made me happy
when I would see people on fire
in Vietnam on the TV.
I liked to believe the unburned people
would rush where people were burning
and the world would stir with motion.
I have believed a lot of things,
which I think about now
watching the trees
waiting
to see if some wind will come
and let them move their leaves.

## Pentecost II

This girl who made an F
breaks down in my office. Tears
as sudden and perfect as stupidity,
exhausting as the red light
you can't un-run once the car
is a heap of scrap, the rearview cleaves
the skull between the eyes, and bones protrude
or penetrate the lungs.

Who would have guessed
the errant commas and fused
clauses could cause such
trauma or I be clumsy as
unparallel structures or the laws
of motion snatching glances at
her anguish from my condescending throne
high above the ineptitude of her grammar?

I'm well aware not every subject
needs a predicate:::regret:::regret
can't untwist steel. Wishing
she wasn't here, I am guilty
of a crude and masculine insensitivity.
But as I dole out tissues from the box
on my desk, she is the one
to say she's sorry.
"Sorry sorry sorry so sorry."
*Mea culpas*
leaking on the scene like gasoline,
and my pedantic indifference
is the cigarette

flicked
in the dripping wreckage.

At last her stricken body stops
convulsing, the ambulance
of fact arrives
like shock with its false and alarming calm:
"Me and my boyfriend just broke up."
Her tears aren't wasted on a comma
splice at all, instead they are spent
on fragments she calls
three wasted years.

> Wasted. Life.
> Wasted affection and.
> Humiliating sex.

She tells me this and asks
what more she might have done
to keep that wreck from happening.
I wish for a grammar native to her need,
a tongue to anoint her head with flame:

> *Moon splinters pain into a thousand equators.*
> *Sun hangs from night on a slender wish.*

# Pentecost III—Whitsunday

From ribs and keel of our capsized ark,
we dangle red crêpe tongues of flame.
The kids are making bright red kites
to test the Spirit's gusty force.
Red-cushioned pews, and kneelers red,
red the wine we sip today,
and red his blood.

Three thousand Passovers have passed,
two thousand Pentecosts, and still
the violent wind descends—O welcome it—
amid the din of this chaotic world,
Babel of zeal and cries for blood.

Familiar symbols fill again, lift us
through forms beyond all forms,
all totems of the numinous: the garments white,
the bitter herbs and slaughtered lamb, star
and cross and crescent moon, lotus, rose,
and wheel, transforming Shiva, yin and yang,
cobra rearing above the brows.

*Lord, gather in one buoyant boat all*
*who seek you by whatever sign, whatever name.*
Amen. Now go in peace to love and serve.

Blessed, dismissed, out into the wilderness
of judges and thieves we take our children
to launch their kites. We see the red wings rise
from spools of string. We smile on all these little ones,
the fruit of passion best in us and ours to raise.

What gusts will lift us up as we raise them?
Will fire we strike consume or save?

Today the sun anoints both us and them.
They seem to see that heaven within themselves
and shout their wonder at the gift of wind.

# Ordinary Time after Pentecost
## A Thousand Petals

## Saint Barnabus

This this this pair of praying mantises,
ecstatic fractal, comes to a leafy limb
in the impulse of emanation
to serve the violent beauty of gestation.

A self that pledges both doing and being
to missionary devotion
sets out, in the ordinary way of seeing,
through a universe terrible and fallen.

Deep inside the darkness
of its hiding, the light of adoration
reveals the scandal of incarnation,
love infinitely and incessantly filling.

Here in this light—all-consumed
and all-consuming—receiver, giver, given
are three thirds of every feast,
the particles of one Person.

And here, sacramentally digesting,
this this this pair of mantises, exemplum of creation,
prays in the frothy sanctity of sacrifice,
in the perfect integrity of consummation.

# The Holy Trinity

Walnut slips from its husk
   gravity   earth   rain
How shall I learn devotion?

## Corpus Christi

They ask me why
I go to the woods.

How can I explain
a pine cone
or whippoorwill
or a thousand
blossoms
on a mountain path?

Only in the presence
of one I love
can I leave my need
for pardon.

# The Nativity of John the Baptist

When I fear I have done wrong,
when I heed those who are less than wise,
when I forget transcendence
    and kneel in the meanings of color and shadow,
when I tell lies to my soul,
I seek out water, I follow its charm—a river, a stream,
a lake with its springs and currents.

See how it offers life
as it flawlessly flows and forms
to the shape of this world, the contours of land, the urge of earth,
hear how it sings under the sun
of endless evaporation.

# The Sacred Heart

Dissection teaches our hands in ways books and software cannot. We are all built to a common plan, but the details are different.

> —anonymous anatomy professor

In the cadaver room
I held a heart
the size of a football.
It was stiff with formaldehyde,
very, very cold,
and motionless.

How much must a man have to love
to grow a heart so big?

Oh, I know what you are thinking:
it was obesity and disease
that swelled it into silence.
Doubtless you have read the texts
on myocardial infarction,
congestive heart failure.  There have been studies,
refereed, in famous journals
on congenital afflictions.

But I am thinking of a man
who sat on sunset bluffs alone
and lacked a priest's or poet's words
to chant his wonder,
who fed cats in lieu of wife or child

to hold and whisper to,
who watched the news
on Christmas Eve
and lacked the notes to sing
or chords to strum away
the thick sorrow gathering
beneath his sternum.
Might not sentiment, unexpressed,
stuff a heart to bursting?

Note well the valves
and chambers of this organ,
cut from the body that encased it.
Read the map-like veins
and arteries beneath the pericardium.
See how the bloodless aorta gapes
like a plastic mouth,
as though to whisper, sing, or kiss.

# Saint Peter and Saint Paul, Apostles

After closing the tavern
we drove to the big bridge
and sat on the tailgate
listening to the water
singing on the pilings.

The air was so still he said
the wind must be sleeping.
I said I should be sleeping.
He said he should be sleeping.
We went on listening.

He said just listen
to the song of the water
against the bridge. I said yeah
that's really something.
We listened a minute.

Then yawning he added
you know that song
is as much the song
of the bridge
as it is of the water.

# Saint Thomas, Apostle

Jesus said, "Whoever has come to know the world has discovered the body, and whoever has discovered the body, of that person the world is not worthy.

—*Gos. Thom.* 80 (NHC II, 2)

## 1. The Certainty of Doubt

That gust, his breath flying
from his body, lifted a hood
from over my head. Clarity!
The long-sought certainty
breaking through at last.
A revelation of negation.

He spoke so much of light.
The wilderness is dark
through which we pass to science,
attain at last the faith to believe
the witness of our eyes.
When we arrive we know
we wanted to be blind.

Truth mocks
a thousand false messiahs,
itself immune from mockery.
His hands, which touched to heal,
in the end held only lies.
Blessed be the lies
that lead to truth.

Whatever it destroys
the fire that burns away illusions
lights the way.
The lesson of his encrypted flesh
surpasses all beatitudes
of the charming deceiver.
Let his ossuary be my altar
on which I burn no sacrifice.

He knew that all I yearn for
is the truth. I would still
have followed him to death
if he had truly taught
that verily death is truth.
It was only truth I sought.

Let the mad disciples rave
in their upper room.
I have my creed, they wander still
in the darkness of faith.
What I saw I know I saw.
Enough to know.
No hand can ever again
lead me away from truth.


## 2. Compound Fracture

Inside the pipe the cowboy reins himself to half a ton of fury.
Boot heels dig into muscle as the chute opens.
That centaur slams against the gate with the force of a bullet.

All in the arena hear the tib/fib fracture, hear the silence of
the rider, just a boy again, now that he is horseless,
the gelding just a gelding, escorted to fodder by the pickup men.

When medics reach their patient he is gritting his teeth in the dirt,

writing. The bone has ripped through sock.
One of us vomits.

We have to cut his ropers off to immobilize the fracture.
That's when the boy begins to curse.
I never touched his wound,

but when he clenched my hand against his pain,
I sensed the unseen aura of his body.
Its perfection, permanence, and power.


## 3. The Zealot

The hand I lost in the war
still clenches and brawls,
slaps the prisoner
in the interrogation room,
squeezes the cold steel trigger.
Attached to the pride
of pain and power,
it clutches violence.

Let it go.

      With my other hand
I tie my shoe with patience.
I spear the needle's eye with thread
to mend the tear
in what I left behind.
I raise my son and daughter
on my shoulders.
I love my wife
in ways we never dreamed of loving.

You only need one hand
to pull yourself through sand
to solid ground, whole at last.

I lost my hand in the war.
I lost my whole right arm.

When it was gone
I found growing from the charred shoulder,
all bone and blood,
the original of every arm.
It had been there all along,
outstretched and holding in its palm
a shining nugget—that emptiness
that is the only teacher of the heart.


## 4. Holy of Holies

From heel to crown, I followed the nerve
of his rising to the temples of Shiva and Kali.
I saw they were made of mist,
the same as the walls of Solomon.

You will not find my bones in the Himalayas
nor my ashes in the Ganges.
Look for me in the wood, under a stone,
in the breath of the tiger.

Gaze through the scales of your eyes
as you sing with the heart of a cobra.
Under the lintel of doubt,
you pass to the holy of holies.

# Saint Mary Magdalene

Chris and Debbie, four years old,
played underneath her mother's house.
They colored beams, built roads in the dirt.
Her mother's friends would come and go.
One day she took off all her clothes:
"Girls do this with boys they like."
Slender pilings held the whole house up.
Spell of dust and spider webs.

Chris and Debbie, six years old.
At school the playground boys played tag:
"You're it you're it you've got Debbie's germs."
Her dirty clothes she seldom changed,
her long unruly hair reeked grease and smoke.
She took their curses, returned a smile,
soon learned to please as she knew how,
and hid inside her nakedness.

I've known so many Magdalenes.
Some women see
there's no such thing as lesser love
so conjure as all witches do with all they have—
vapors of a boiling brew
made of sweet and bitter herbs,
wild flesh, and hairy wings.
Oh, let me taste!

Debbie and Chris, now forty-six.
Seven times her longing love
possessed and then deserted her.
Seven times he bought her back.

Her lovers cannot comprehend,
they have no eyes,
so make of her what they desire.
He sees her as she really is.

# Saint James, Apostle

Where is the forgiveness tree?
You will not find it growing
in garden or rain forest.

It sprouts in arid wilderness
in ancient sediments caliche hard
beneath the ever-shifting sand.

A seed will drift through wind-blown dust
to drop in some unlikely cleft
like sun-cracked lips or a cut on the hand.

There is no water here.
Like a parasite this little seed
needs human blood.

Once it roots in the wounded earth
it grows and grows,
slender sapling strong as iron,

until it bears a single bloom
that pollinates itself to yield a single fruit
black as a living heart stuffed with bile.

The vision of this one ripe plum
like an aborted giant horrifies,
its smell disgusts.

Reach, beloved, through bone-bare limbs
with both your arms
to pluck that body down.

Take and eat.
Feast, feast.
Feast on the bitterest flesh of earth.

## Saint Martha

Do with me what gasoline does with an engine,
combustion and the steel push of piston. Let the turn
of the wheel reveal to the highway
how carbon makes life in the universe.

Do with me what the keyboard does with fingers,
naked ribs of scales and chords, the tickling
and gliding polygamy of touch inviting the throat
of the soloist to the hymn of the spheres.

Do with me what the cardinal does with the aspen,
splashing late afternoon with audacious hues,
whistling, purring, chirring sacred syllables to wind
until sky knows itself again.

Do with me what the full moon does with a meadow.
Surely a generous mist will rise, and the light
that we make will remind the canyons
how vast is the night.

Do with me what the threshold does with the room.
Do with me what dawn does with east, east with dawn.
Do with me what words do with a poet.
Whatever blood does with the body, do it.

## The Transfiguration

I do not believe in death without resurrection. If they kill me, I will be resurrected in the Salvadoran people.

—Oscar Romero

The day Oscar Romero tasted the soil
of El Salvador, a woman
filled a basket with vegetables.

The sun kissed her face
and the face of the lettuce
with equal passion.

Little insects hid
in the crevices made by the leaves
and the sun could not caress them.

For the time it took
the body of Oscar Romero to fall
there was no fear in all the land.

The day Oscar Romero looked up
from behind the altar, he could taste
the soil of El Salvador.

Unknown to each other, he
and the woman, busy that morning with seeds,
held for an instant a single thought.

They remembered the gardens of childhood,
how the stems resisted
when they pulled the squash and corn,

and how the earth stubbornly held the roots,
reluctant to lose even one
ordinary miracle.

## Saint Clare of Assisi

The body is designed for benediction.
Mirrored smiles and mantras of endearment
tune the breath and nourish cells that fight
off stress and inflammation. Flesh flourishes
in the meeting of eyes, in the joyous communion
of creaturely glances of tender affection.
The solitary knows that even chastity
needs arms to hold our virgin devotion. Truly
all who seek him here find God in the body.
Thus we are people of the road, made
of matter and madly in love with molecules
that dance to a canticle of blessing.
This is the larger knowing and letting go
that some call death, that we call living.

# The Assumption of the Blessed Virgin Mary

Adoration raises the blue jay
from elder limb to the highest ring
of the sky god's realm.
The wind is singing to everyone.

If you would seek the goddess lost
for centuries to find
inside yourself
the sanctity of all,

ask what did I do,
what task,
more than any daughter
born by blood and water.

I was young, and I conceived.
I chose to bear the child in me.
I tenderly held that son and loved
the thorny beauty of the rose.

# The Queenship of the Blessed Virgin Mary

Wherever you are, take off your shoes.

The Presence
is more than a mountaintop moment,
more than a mystic epiphany of a chosen few,
more than transcendent assumption—*yes! yes!*—of immaculate one.

The Presence
is plain old love, down and dirty.
It happens now

in the desires and diseases of the body,
sometimes through the worst intentions,
always in the best,

in the exuberance and mess of shared life
with all its fluid loss and joy,
all agony and embracing,

in the willful needing and reluctant releasing,
bird flight and leaf fall,

in despair, which dies,
in hope, which knows no death.

# Saint Bartholomew, Apostle

The free-ranging deer
savor the figs
of my brother's trees,
his gift to the little ones.

Shovel and hoe rest
against the greenhouse.

Unfit for war,
the old tiller
spreads out
on a canvas sail
in a hundred pieces.

Below the feeder
hanging from an oak,
ancient of days,
a squirrel salvages
sunflower seeds
spilled by
a generous jay.

We watch from the porch.
Our wine is sweet.
This evening is sweet.
It brings no fear.
It tells no lies.

# Saint Monica

**1.**

Momma took the boys to church
in the red Impala.
The hymns she sang all day
fell on our food
like manna
as she cooked a big family dinner.

With a bowl in her lap while the baby slept,
she made ambrosia.
Cherries, orange, banana, pecans.
The apple peel,
unbroken,
coiled around her hand.

**2.**

Down on the border
the babbling, ice-hearted
generals
are building two mountains
higher than Babel
on the plain of Har Meggido.

One is made from the nipples
of nursing mothers.
One is made from the lips
of their nursing children.

They tower above two continents
with the Valley of Death between them.



3.

My mother taught me,
"Kindness is everything."
So at age 63 I find myself
in Tornillo, Texas, with millions
of mothers and fathers and children
in the shadow

of the Davis Mountains
marching for mothers and fathers
and children,
separated and caged,
aliens in an ailing country
that offers them no welcome.



4.

Not far from here
we go sometimes
to watch the stars
from the great observatory,
high in the blackest air,
mountains sacred to the Mescalero.

Today, Father's Day,
we stand
in the mid-year sun
in the season of Lupus, the Wolf,
under the scales of Libra
and know the stars are watching us.

5.

Driving east toward home
and my waiting children
through mountains the white men named
for a man of war
who became the Confederate president,
I ponder my nation's history.

Gentle Mother,
won't you intercede for us
to keep the wolf at bay, to tip the scales,
to fill us up
with fruit of loving-kindness
for the sake of every child.

# Saint Augustine

A girl sits on a bench
between her grandparents

in the apple-tree bloom
of her femininity.

With her feet pulled up on the bench
she is in a fetal position.

Using her bony knees as a table
she plays a game on her cell phone.

Suddenly her hand
brushes away from her face

a wisp of hair—quick,
graceful parabola of pure being.

How can I express
or repudiate my longing?

Where shall I find a love more worthy
of all that I am burning to be?

# The Passion of Saint John the Baptist

She danced, and the prophet
swooned on the floor inside me.
Of course I called for a sword,

and the blood of that beheading
was sweet, I tell you,
as a thousand hallelujahs of honeysuckle.

I've read every testament and sutra.
I've heard the *adhan* of Confucius calling
and the hemlock tongue of meditation.

I sat on the white lotus of AUM
with my mind drained of all but Tao.
Samadhi, Satori, Ein Sof, Union

with God beyond any God. All
the petals of the universe are peeled.
I have passed with every patriarch,

reverent, through the cleft of covenant,
and now I know the same as any king.
The nakedest truth Love ever revealed

howls in the music of her moving
and is the verse the prophets sing
as they sleep in silence.

# Saint Joseph of Arimathea

In Big Bend National Park
wind ripples the face
of an igneous sea, sunlight
ripens the rim
to a barren crust.

From Persimmon Gap
to Boquillas Canyon,
every rock reveals
the history of earth.
Break one open. See
how the hardest matter
is kin to stars.

When your soul becomes a stone
hollow it out, hide
a god there, then wait
a few days to see what happens.

## Saint Nicodemus

As they came from their mother's womb, so shall they go again,
naked as they came

> —Eccl 5:15a (NRSV)

I went as a moral machine to see him, with my faith
in rule and consequence, cause and effect.
He invited me into his archetype.
It was something alluring, but self-destroying.
I fled in the night.

I went again, to watch his passion, still believing
in the iron mechanics of flesh.
Watching, it seemed I had seen it before.
It had the usual ending. As Sabbath drew near,
they gave us the corpse.

Washing his body I remembered bathing my sons
as they entered the world. I touched his lowliness.
The words he spoke that night returned.
At last I could hear them.
This machine became human.

# The Nativity of the Blessed Virgin Mary

for Sarah

Born this day after long night's fear,
Love's labor, and the thrill of blood,
A girl to make her father glad
And bring the glow of morning here.

Whatever nourishes the new flesh there
Upon the pliant softness of the breast,
Pray, give her laughter, a place to rest,
And cunning to confound despair.

# The Exaltation of the Holy Cross

When three years old I swallowed a nail.
It made a milky "1" on the X-ray screen.
It made a twisting journey through my guts.
It came out clean.

> Breath of love
> O breath of Love
> I ate the nails
> that fastened you
> to elder wood
> no less a lamb
> than I myself.
> Such little wounds
> they made in me
> healing as they went.

First the fact and then the meaning of the fact.
First the image then the symbol.
Lash falls on skin.
Nail driven into bone.
Crown of thorns, the pierced side, the bitter wine.
We had no theological thoughts,
no exegeses or Christologies in mind
the day we fetched him down.
There was only the bloody body of a man.

The night before, without ears to hear
we heard him speak. Our eyes grew heavy
as he prayed. But when they came,
our thoughts were filled with swords,
we felt the iron in our veins.

Yet he was calm, calm
as the unstirred water of Siloam.

In spring red flowers
spatter the Syrian mountainsides.
We call them Blood of Martyrs.

One mild, sweet Indian summer,
in the chancel of Holy Angels
below the cedar crucifix
I stole my first kiss.
The rosy flush of cheeks,
warm breath, wet lips,
the thrill of sin not sin.
I have hung in that moment ever since,
the blood come down.

Down the street called Straight
to the Chapel of Paul
up to Ninevah I went.
Beside our boat,
beneath the waves,
the hump-backed shadow
stalking me.
I stopped for nothing evil on the way.
Ummayad Mosque
(Tower of Issa,
Yahyah's head in emerald light,
the tomb of chivalrous Salah al-Din,
the Lion-Hearted yielding
to the Righteousness of Faith)
swallowed me down
then spat me out.
In Bab Touma I shopped
in the gold and carpet *suq*.
I bought a scarf and tablecloth
to send back home.
*Talata shabab—*

they made me tea
then bargained for my cloak.
My confessor says
I must forgive.
Habibi, habibi,
why do you hide your face from me?
What is that dragon down under the sea?
Little Deema
with your sad black eyes,
how could I know
your sad whale-song,
your barren road?
We who never labored sing.

From the land of the living they tore me out.

> *crux simplex*
> *crux commissa*
> *crux immissa*
> *crux decusata*

Stretch out, O tender shoot, let go,
let go of all in you that is not love.
I seal my covenant with a kiss,
I did not open once my mouth.
Father, are you not satisfied?
In him the nails are ladder rungs.
In him my blood and bones divine.

To Pilate we went and begged.
*Here is your king.*
We bit the nails that bound him there.
We felt in his corpse a pent-up power.
*We have no king but Ceasar,*
*take him away!*
See
the broken bread, the wine poured out,
the billions you have crucified.

To the city of peace

the Sabbath comes.
The *azan* calls the evening prayer.
Where is Adam's skull? O where?
I follow the sweating Jesuits
down the Dolorous Avenue
stumbling thirst and blood
to Calvary
where nuns are praying,
where tourists are posing.

In Azizieh I saw
the holy cross, I saw
the pretty blue figurines
of the Virgin Mother.
The tanks of the regime
have come against
the grim mujahidin.
I crawled from the Marionite Church,
to Jamia al-Tawahid I crawled,
a sword in my guts.
*ana l-Haqq*
Many the tombs
throughout al-Sham,
many the babes
of Bethlehem.
Who can speak of our descendants?
Woman and whale are one.

On the Mount of Olives
they spat on me.
They took my love,
they made me weep.
Across a valley of graves I looked
to the Dome of the Rock.

To some deserted place I go.
The old stars gleam against the night.
The eyes of Cetus fill with light,

fill and cross their brilliant beams.
Among the twisted olive trees
I sweat and groan.
The torches and the judgment come.
Night wears darkness in the minds of men.
In silent rooms throughout the town
the Word, the Word enfleshed.
Somewhere two thieves are waiting for the day.
Somewhere a mother grieves her son.
I am the vine, and on this vine
the dawn's first thread of light descends.
That earth-bound bird the rooster crows.

The tree leans on mystery.
   No one has climbed it.
      Everyone climbs it.

The idea of the tree dies
   in the realization of the tree.
      The tree leans on nothing.

This is my tree, elder tree.
   In my own skull I planted it.
      I raised it ring by ring.

In naked joy I meander among the quadrants.
   You have your own tree.
      It is the same tree.

# Our Lady of Sorrows

Both in the past and now, I set forth only this: suffering and the end of suffering.
—The Buddha


So many days begin
with an egg. So simple:
shell breaks on porcelain,
thumb punctures membrane.

Pancakes for the dawn of my wedding,
whisking egg and milk together.
On the morning of a death quite
unexpected I made an omelet.

The first day of school and the last.
Quiche for the big promotion.
The first kiss and the last kiss.
She made soufflé on Christmas.

Some days we find next to the yolk
a bit of blood. The boys on the bridge
were drowning a cat. That day.
The day I took him away

from their cruelty and carried him home.
Again that morning, a morning
like others, he ran in front of the car.
He was euthanized in my arms.

One day we wake and want eggs.
A plane crashes.
A friend we thought would be with us forever
is gone forever.

My children one by one arrived
on days I stirred the eggs.
Something I never knew was in me hatching.
Call it love. Or need. Something.

Today, breaking the eggs, alone,
picking a bit of shell from the bowl,
I see it outlasts the birth
of their leaving.

## Saint Matthew, Apostle and Evangelist

I dearly loved the clink of gold on gold.
Is that a sin? This metal when I bite
it tastes of stardust. After all it comes
from outer space. That's where our luminous
great Caesar lives forever and a day.
Therefore, you must admit this gold is his.
It says so on the very coin you pay
your taxes with. Why kick against the goads?
Just think of all you buy when you contribute
your fair share to the internal revenue.
The Roman Peace is not exactly free.
Don't you appreciate the first-class roads
and aquifers? Who keeps the riffraff off
the streets? There cannot be society
without police. Stop griping then. Pay up.
Of course I kept a small percentage back
to compensate me for my time and trouble.
I heard a preacher preaching how God wants
me rich as Solomon, how of blessing
prosperity is the one sure sign.
So where's my crime?

Indeed, I thought this way, one time.
Then a homeless man said, "Follow me."
I followed.

Can you see why?

## The Archangels
## or
## Michaelmas

The Cosmos hums in the quiver of creating,
in every arrow of atoms transforming.
Listen to the AUM of First and Last, and sing
the hymn of all new flesh, the utterance
of energy, particle, wave, cells dividing,
stars exploding, infinity ever toward itself expanding.
This is Word proclaimed, All in all,
already perfect, always perfecting.

# Saint Thérèse of the Child Jesus

Ever since the creation of the world his eternal power and divine nature, invisible though they are, have been understood and seen through the things he has made.

> —Rom 1:20 (NRSV)

Bird song delights you on an April morning—
the sunny oak, iris and clover flaunting their divinity,
and even the muddy pond fills with infinity.

On such a day
it is not hard to feel the kingdom close.

Yet more is in the air
than scent of bee-crazed nectar.
Vultures swirl above the carrion.
Can you smell high heaven?

Rabbit and coyote
enact their ritual of necessity.

Parasite, bacteria, virus,
a black hole swallowing planets like plankton—
can you fathom the whole in your science?

Can you listen to your body as it weakens
and hear the humming of eternal power?
Can you see the holy image in a corpse
as sure as in its birth and its begetting?

When you are ready, look full in the face of this love,
dive into nature, down and down
until bursting.

Just when you are drowning, breathe deeply, die
in the beauty
and praise it with giddy alleluias
from your deepest being.

# The Holy Guardian Angels

One of us said
let's sleep on the beach
and love in the glow
of Cassiopeia.
Kids holding hands,
we walked on the shore.
Later that night,
like some B movie
where nature attacks,
the beach came alive
with crustaceans, the tide
dredged up the smell of dead fish,
and way off-shore
an oily green glow
made the night look sick.
A stiff wind rose
and blowing grit
made our sex
a sanding of planks.
In the morning
a cold rain fell.
We could kindle no fire
so slogged to the bait shop
for rancid coffee
and pickled eggs.
The 60s convulsed
and then bled out.
The 70s fell
like acid rain.
Somehow we came
back from all the wars

we went to die in
and made a few kids
who made a few kids.
Their century dawned
in angry fire,
leaving us all but dead.
How we kept our livers
and stuck to each other
through all that grit
is anyone's guess.
We set out with this idea
of a life together,
of what marriage is,
but took instead
what was given,
held the beach,
and lived.

# Saint Francis of Assisi

This homeless, holy fool,
jester of Me and Mine,
surfs the dumpster.

Retrieving
with a lunatic trill of delight
half a discarded burger,

he retires to the park,
Sultan of Santa Fe,
Lord of the Manor.

He tosses his bread on the grass,
belches baritone poems
to the wind and sun,

to the geese and squirrels,
and cackles of Tet and Saigon
as of something hilarious.

His body stinks.
His bristles beg for a razor.
The war destroyed him.

He rejoices in nothingness,
some glory that we are too poor
to perceive, too dumb to discover.

The opulence of his poverty
illuminates our need.
Of course we avoid him.

## Our Lady of the Rosary

At the kitchen table
my son is solving calculus problems while
I count the beats in lines of pentameter.
Who knows which of us will be first
to reach the stars?

## Saint Luke, Evangelist

The one who tells the story becomes the story. The story becomes the one who tells it.

The story came to me out of a cloud. I absorbed the rain, and being a man of science, arranged the drops according to time and logic. The plot needed conflict, crisis, climax—pyramid of all good stories. The resolution demanded a sequel.

Within the margins of poetic license, never forgetting the tedium and prejudice of history, I bound my narrative to the characters as they were given. Meaning arrived through the weather of spectacle on the gusts of their motivation, wind you can feel with every thought on your temple.

The Mother that bore Asclepius and Hippocrates also conceived Homer. Despite our materialism, empiricism, our mastery of logic, we Greeks are no strangers to magic and fantasy. We love our gods, demigods, and de-mons, embodiments of elemental forces. Sea-stranded isles with monsters and witches. Archetype and allegory flair in the myths of our people, in the songs of our minstrels.

I write within this tradition. All writing is for edification. The feral hero of the Myrmidons, a figure of Wrath, drags his own body in the dust behind his chariot. After the war, Resourcefulness (the man of Ithaca) refuses immortality, kills all the suitors, pauses to clean up the gore, and spends a happy night with his wife, symbol of Gnosis, the boon of every journey. Is that not edifying?

Let us never forget that the Muses are daughters of Memory. The goddess who breathes in the poet cares not a whit for the literal. Truth alone is alive. What is truth? I understand your fetish for proof. I, too, am a man of science. Science is forever gestating. I am also a poet. Poetry crosses dangerous oceans to reach the ports of the psyche.

Therefore, sweet Theophilus, taste my story as spun from the lips of divinity, let it swallow you whole, and digest in the belly of remembrance.

The story comes alive in you.

And you come alive in the story.

# Saint James, the Lord's Brother

Sweating from the hay fields
in the mouth of a summer evening
we bought our Miller at the Buckhorn
and drank along the river.
The moon watched itself rising
in the calm of a deep pool,
certain of its setting
as the bottles were sure of their emptying.
The five of us, boys really,
stuck the dead soldiers neck down
in the ground
and stoned them.

Our first knowing
is the science of breaking.
First we break the water of our birth.
We break the toys we're given.
Soon we break each other.
We throw a rock to break the moon
to pieces in the water. Meanwhile, the moon,
however fractured its reflection
in the river, is not afraid,
and the bottles that we shatter
sparkle in a mound of shards
as they catch the moonlight.

## Saint Simon and Saint Jude, Apostles

The beauty that is truth
is often neither beautiful

nor true. The truthful
beautiful sucks

mangoes from the bloody
battlefield, takes the kids

for a Sunday drive buckled
in the urn on sharks' teeth.

Pearls come alive
in the death of the mussel like

the masterpiece pried
from pain. And there, there in

a wash of fluorescent
objectivity you see

the coroner opening
the child's chest like

the kingdom of heaven.
The heart, a pearl, a mango—

*how beautiful!*
*how true!*

# All Hallows' Eve

I made the mask
of my face the mask
of the face that I mask

The face I mask
is the mask
of the face of the mask

# All Saints

for Troy Reeves

And I heard a voice from heaven saying, "Write this: Blessed are the dead who from now on die in the Lord."

— Rev 14:13a (NRSV)

A half moon, waning through
      the bare oak branches, spins
            a labyrinth of shadows

around my heels. Last night's
      masquerade has left
            on Oxford Street a trail

of Coke cans, apple cores,
      candy wrappers, dropped
            in the swirl of red oak leaves.

As I walk below its roost,
      a single mourning dove
            awakes in a flutter of wings.

The cold caresses my bones.
      Winter stares me in the face,
            assurance of winter sleep.

What is that sleep that waits?
      Today I'll make my rounds.

In nursing homes, the old

and sick will see my collar
            and be comforted.
                        *Father Bob is here, and while*

*he's here my death dare not*
            *come near.* They'll take the wine-
                        dipped host upon their tongues.

Dead eyes will stare inside
            the masks some wear to scare
                        the graying priest (*Here is*

*your death!*), but even they
            can mouth *Our Father* when
                        the prayer begins. From there

I'll visit Agnes in
            the Shannon cancer ward.
                        I'll smile and bless my young

parishioner, then cross
            myself and sit beside
                        her bed. Leukemia

has made her head a skull,
            and I will praise her courage
                        and her dainty art—the pumpkins,

witches, brooms she's drawn,
            the black cats cut from black
                        construction paper, stars

and angels haloed with gold
            and silver glitter on
                        the same black sheets. I'll hold

her hand. I'll pray
            while she vomits in a pan.
                        Last night, behind each mask

of evil and decay—ghost
            or ghoul, skeleton
                        or zombie—was a child

with an appetite for sweets.
            One little witch, too scared
                        and shy to cry her spell

when at my door she stood
            for treats, hugged her mother's
                        legs and hid. Is this

the face of winter sleep?
            Is this the face of that
                        momentous sleep that sparks

such grief and dread so big?
            Here in the littered street
                        before the break of day

the moonlight summons all
            the witnesses: Stephen,
                        Peter, Paul, Bartholomew

and Jude; sweet Philomena,
            princess, who took the only
                        Emperor for suitor;

Agnes, whom they dragged
            naked to a brothel before
                        the wood refused to burn;

Engratia and Valentine,
            the hermit brothers of hills;

the printer Tyndale, Fisher,

Thomas More, who down
    the gallows shifted for himself,
        and Thomas Cranmer reaching

with his bad right hand to pluck
    his recantations from the flame;
        the Tonkin Martyrs, young

and old, unknown and known,
    whose bodies—decomposed—
        now silt the Mekong River;

my Bonhoeffer, dear disciple
    of Flossenburg, who hung
        at dawn above the snarling teeth

of curs; San Salvador's
    beloved Romero—Father
        Oscar learned when young

to bevel, saw, and plane
    then took the level of the world
        to frame a perfect door.

Thousands upon thousands
    more, of every age
        and faith. Here stands the lover

Hallaj, Truth ablaze,
    and Thich Quang Duc, who lit
        the whole wide world with just

the tiny candle of
    his flesh, and Shanti Kali,
        whose blood the Queen of Queens

reveres. Here all the dead
　　　who died by fire, by sword,
　　　　　by noose, by teeth of beasts

amass from time and shadow
　　　to greet me in the figure
　　　　　of a bashful child, and all

their voices gather into one.
　　　They whisper, *Death*.
　　　　　The word that burns:

*Death, Death, Death.*
　　　They are savoring *Death*
　　　　　in the frigid dark. Sweet *Death*,

we coo, radiant on lips,
　　　on tongues, delicious *Death*
　　　　　in the milky hemlock breath

of dawn.

# The Commemoration of the Faithful Departed

Along the blue Zambezi,
the villages come
and dip their buckets.
Sweet Zambezi water
drawn from every mile
to quench the thirst
of jungle, mountain, plain.
Its loops and lakes
consider nothing
of nations, boundaries.
The water is the guest
of the land—watershed,
catchment, basin, bed—
returning hospitality
to its inhabitants.
Here the water dances,
throwing back the light
to a grateful sky.
Down the stream a little,
rivulets curl
in the shadows of rock.
And where the land
breaks, the river sings
in thunder.  Farther on,
the confluence
slows in ponderous black pools.
A desert comes alive,
answering its invitation.
In the bog the water
is brackish with scales
of centuries, the claws

and hooves of mammals,
teeth of reptiles,
excrement and chum.
From high to low the songs
of this current keep
her time. The melody
of headwaters, dirges of
the depths, alto-tenor
interludes of rapids,
a chorus of a thousand
tributaries along the course
all harmonize in reverence.
Life is listening.
The fruit of every tree
no matter how sweet
or how it stinks, each bird
and viper, lizard, rat
along the shores, every fish
and amphibian, all
that slithers and crawls, insect
or worm, arthropod,
parasite, all that takes its life
from the water
is claiming beauty original,
terror on its own terms,
design unique, benign,
interconnected relevance
engendered by
a single mind,
the mind of mud and cloud.

# The Presentation of the Blessed Virgin Mary

Without wake or eulogy,
  I lie in my grave.
An earthy sea, enshrouding me,
  Has hid the face of Love.

Unexpected vision comes
  To the one born blind.
So the light of morning dawns
  In my benighted mind.

Anointing rays of Mercy break
  My night with gentle might.
My heart, once staked to dreadful dark,
  Begins to beat with life.

Its breaking breaks the spell of sin
  That over me was cast.
First forms I see, then living men,
  As I awake at last.

Illumined by celestial beams
  Of tender love and wise,
Oppressèd earth in beauty gleams
  To my delighted eyes—

All the more to love the One
  That I half loved before,
To face this day the risen sun,
  To see forever more.

# Christ the King

Christ the King Sunday
at the Carmelite Hermitage
near Christoval.

A sudden shower.
Rain plays timpani
on the skull of this world.

The bearded, shaved-pated monks,
famous for singing,
raise a fanfare for their Lord.

The bony land a chorus of voices:
live oak and limestone,
hawk and juniper, dove and deer.

Sheep and cattle in distant pastures
evoke the manger
with their ruminant worship.

Rain has polished the statue of Mary,
Stations of the Cross,
gleaming in the mid-day light.

Among the sticks and stones
of that grove, a snake
has come to bask,

striped with sunbeams on its side and spine,
coiled,
a crown for the King.

# Recessional: Anatomy and Atonement

I know a person in Christ who fourteen years ago was caught up to the third
heaven—whether in the body or out of the body I do not know; God knows.
And I know that such a person—whether in the body or out of the body I do not
know; God knows—was caught up into Paradise and heard things that are not to
be told, that no mortal is permitted to repeat.

   —2 Cor 12:2–4 (NRSV)


A shelf of blue encyclopedias
anchored the lone bookcase
in the seven-room house of my childhood.
Before I was able to read,
the entry for "anatomy"
gave me a map of my body.

In the beginning, there was a skeleton,
onto which I could then fold over
a succession of plastic pages
imprinted in living colors, hieroglyphs
for each of the body's systems.
Male and female He created them.

The stomach and liver hover above
the serpentine coils of intestines.
Red and blue tributaries
lead from and to the heart.
The wiry schematics of nerves like vines
branch from the spinal axis
to deliver the brain's commands

to every limb and member.
Those twin pink bellows, the lungs,
connect by pipes to the nostrils,
where (I remember thinking)
breath first entered Adam.

Meanwhile in my father's old sea chest,
he'd buried a secret treasure.
A volume as weighty as the family Bible:
World War II in pictures.
I looked at the book in secret,
the Eve in me yearning,
certain because forbidden
that it hid some alchemical knowledge.
Bodies in flight and battle, bleeding and burning.
Acres and acres of corpses.

Every month in *Reader's Digest*,
where laughter is the best medicine,
Joe's spleen and all his relatives,
all the essential organs,
explained their raison d'etre.

On Sundays, engraved upon the altar,
a line in gold letters assured me
GOD IS LOVE.

Where all the bodies of the Body gather
I bear all my questions.
What is the meaning of *Imago Dei*?
What does it mean to be a creature?
Where is psyche abiding
within the channels and chambers
of the animal?
In this cathedral of bone and meat
where are the roots of our virtues?
How will my atoms, dissolved,
reassemble for Doomsday judgment?

Every body mirrors my body
in and beyond our questions,
the bread of our Sunday brunches,
harmony of hymn and liturgy,
reason and vision.

My body mirrors every body,
not living and living, insect and angel.
We have no being
apart from belonging, joined and equal,
a new creation.

With thunder in the mouth of his war wound,
my father, who died in the war, booms out
the recessional. The road from our red doors
leads to a summit beyond religion,
to a shining already ours. From tail to heart,
from heart to crown, the signs are in every cell.

*This is my body*

Our body—Love unveiling,
from the long exile of heart
and mind to life delivered.

*This is my blood*

Our blood—iron and essence,
stream of *hessed*—quick, perfect
in weakness—spirit, creature.